# ALL SORTS of
# Noises

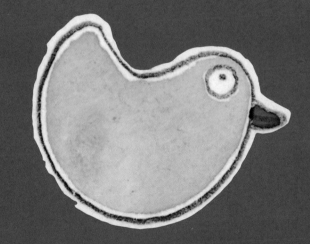

For Robert Dodd. e.d.

Picture Window Books
5115 Excelsior Boulevard
Suite 232
Minneapolis, MN 55416
877-845-8392
www.picturewindowbooks.com

Printed in the United States of America.
First published by Zero to Ten (a member of the Evans Publishing Group)
2A Portman Mansions, Chiltern Street, London W1U 6NR, United Kingdom

**Library of Congress Cataloging-in-Publication Data**

Reidy, Hannah.
All sorts of noises / written by Hannah Reidy ; illustrated by Emma Dodd.
p. cm. — (All sort of things)
Summary: Describes some of the sounds that children hear throughout the day, like kitchen noises, street noises, and nighttime noises.
ISBN 1-4048-1064-1 (hardcover)
[1. Sound—Fiction.] I. Dodd, Emma, 1969- ill. II. Title. III. Series.
PZ7.R27377Alsn 2004
[E]—dc22
2004023874

# ALL SORTS of
# Noises

Written by Hannah Reidy
Illustrated by Emma Dodd

Special thanks to our reading consultant:
Susan Kesselring, M.A.
Literacy Educator
Rosemount-Apple Valley-Eagan (Minnesota) School District

PiCTURE WiNDOW BOOKS
Minneapolis, Minnesota

**Bbring!**

Groan!

Tweet!
Tweet!

Before her eyes are
even open, Eve can hear

4

rustle
rustle

morning noises.

5

Between bites of her breakfast,
Kesia can hear

kitchen noises.

Holding Dad's hand
all the way,
Stuart can hear

Beep! Beep!

Mutter! Mutter!

Vrooom!

Squeak!

Clump!

8

street noises.

Busy with her brush,

10

Brenda can hear playgroup noises.

# Waiting quietly in line,
## Hugh can hear

people noises.

Doctor

Aachoo!

Aachoo!

Lying in the
green grass,
Rosie can hear

14

garden noises.

As her silly sister splashes Dad, Beth can hear **bath-time noises.**

Tired and tucked in tight,
    Nina can hear

after . . .

nighttime noises.

19

what noises do

these things make?

21

# FUN FACTS

 Your ears are still working, even when you are asleep.

 A baby's cry can be louder than a car horn.

 Dogs can hear many more things than people can. Dogs can hear much higher frequencies, which is why they respond to "silent" dog whistles.

 The sound of a snore can be almost as loud as the noise of a drill.

 Nobody knows why, but a duck's quack doesn't echo.

# WORDS TO KNOW

**garden**—a place outside where people grow plants and flowers

**kitchen**—a room in the house where you cook food and eat meals

**morning**—the early part of the day when the sun comes up

**nighttime**—the late part of the day when the sun sets

**noises**—sounds that you can hear

**playgroup**—a group of friends that play together

# TO LEARN MORE

## At the Library

Fox, Mem. *Night Noises*. San Diego: Harcourt Brace Jovanovich, 1989.

Olien, Becky. *Sound*. Mankato, Minn.: Capstone Press, 2003.

Pfeffer, Wendy. *Sounds All Around*. New York: HarperCollins, 1999.

Showers, Paul. *The Listening Walk*. New York: HarperCollins, 1991.

## On the Web

FactHound offers a safe, fun way to find Web sites related to this book.

All of the sites on FactHound have been researched by our staff.

*www.facthound.com*

　1. Visit the FactHound home page.

　2. Enter a search word related to this book, or type in this special code: 1404810641

　3. Click on the FETCH IT button.

Your trusty FactHound will fetch the best Web sites for you!

# INDEX

**Look for all of the books in the All Sorts of Things series:**

All Sorts of Clothes

All Sorts of Noises

All Sorts of Numbers

All Sorts of Shapes

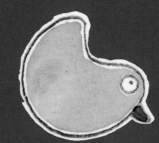